Out of the Ruins

OUT OF THE RUINS

William Johnson

Confluence Press
Lewiston, Idaho

Acknowledgements

Grateful acknowledgement is made to the books and magazines in which these poems, some of them in earlier forms, have appeared or are forthcoming.

EXPRESSIONS: "Dworshak Dam"
FISHTRAP ANTHOLOGY III: "The Elm" (formerly "Stump")
HIGH COUNTRY NEWS: "Steelhead"
IDAHO ENGLISH JOURNAL: "Passage"
IDAHO'S POETRY: A CENTENNIAL ANTHOLOGY: "Wildrose Cemetery"
LEFTBANK: "Snapbeans"
MOTHER EARTH NEWS: "Trout"
NORTHWEST MAGAZINE (THE OREGONIAN): "Suicide Race"
PALOUSE JOURNAL: "On the Palouse"
PETROGLYPH: "Floating the Salmon River"
POETRY: "Cedar"
POETRY NORTHWEST: "Burning the Raspberry Canes," "Coyoteskin," "Fireweed," "Icefishing on Lost Valley Reservoir," "Late Autumn Run," "New Year's Eve," "A Pulling," "Root Cellar"
PRAIRIE SCHOONER: "Hawks," "Out of the Ruins"
QUARTERLY WEST: "Moose"
SNAPDRAGON: "Northern Lights"(formerly "Wigwam Burners")
TALKING RIVER REVIEW: "A Japanese Fisherman on the Henry's Fork," "The Salmon," "Workboots"
WEBER STUDIES: "Chinese Ruins on the Salmon"
WILDERNESS: "Black Lead Mountain"

Thanks to Keith Browning, Okey Goode, Jim Hepworth, Ripley Hugo, Cheryl Johnson, Greg Keeler, Chip Rawlins, and Bill Studebaker who read and commented on earlier drafts of many of these poems. Thanks as well to Brian Kolstad and Katrinka Nelson for their good humor and technical support.

Out of the Ruins Copyright 2000 by William Johnson. All Rights Reserved.
Cover Image Copyright 1999 Photodisc, Inc.
Book design by Brian Kolstad.

Library of Congress Card Number: 99 75095
ISBN: 1-881090-31-0 (paper)
1-881090-34-5 (cloth)

First Edition
04 03 02 01 00   5 4 3 2 1

Published by:
Confluence Press, Inc.
Lewis-Clark State College
500 Eighth Avenue
Lewiston, ID 83501
(208) 799-2336

Distributed by:
Midpoint Trade Books
1263 Southwest Blvd.
Kansas City, KS 66103
(913) 831-2233
Fax (913) 362-7401

for Cheryl, Brendan, Suzanne, and Stephen

Contents

I. Northern Lights

3 Stopping at an Abandoned Farm
4 Morning Work
5 Northern Lights
6 Fort Wright Bridge
7 Trout
8 Root Cellar
9 Quince
10 My Father's Work
11 Girl and Barn: A Photograph, 1931
12 Terminal Ice
13 Letter from Arlington
14 Snapbeans

II. Painting the Trim

17 New Year's Eve
18 Floating the Salmon River
19 Bear in Fog
20 My Daughter's Song
21 At Dworshak Dam
23 Fireweed
24 Burning the Raspberry Canes
25 Bouquet
26 At Sheep Lake During the Gulf War
27 Painting the Trim
28 On Finding a Snapshot of My Children

III. Obsequy for the End of the Century

31	Coyoteskin
32	On the Palouse
33	A Japanese Fisherman on the Henry's Fork
34	Chinese Ruins on the Salmon
35	Icefishing on Lost Valley Reservoir
37	Steelhead
38	Moose
39	Obsequy for the End of the Century
40	The Salmon
41	A Pulling
43	Black Lead Mountain
44	Suicide Race
45	In Mountain Lightning

IV. Out of the Ruins

49	Passage
50	Late Autumn Run
52	The Elm
53	Out of the Ruins
54	Hawks
55	At Fishtrap
56	Workboots
57	Dragging Bottom
58	Cedar
59	Paring My Mother's Nails
60	Wildrose Cemetery

The reality of any joy in the world is indescribable; only in joy does creation take place (happiness, on the contrary, is only a promising, intelligible constellation of things already there); joy is a marvellous increasing of what exists, a pure addition out of nothingness.

—Rilke

. . . we were not born to survive
Only to live

—W.S. Merwin

I. Northern Lights

Stopping at an Abandoned Farm

Only moss knows the echo of their footsteps,
the porch and its broken slats

reminders of the slow claim light makes
tasting the weight of their absence.

In a cupboard mouse-droppings gather,
dark seeds hardening into the future,

and cracked wallpaper buckles into
spring with a faded reckoning of flowers.

If I could read past touching, dust-webs
would name the wind on my fingers.

Hung from a nail by the door, a razorstrap
robs the air of its echo, time like a welt

of light, what the hole in the chimney hoarded
when a junkman hauled out the stovepipe.

From the kitchen she saw the black fist
of a watertank lording it over the barn

and far off poplars scattered the sun
and sometimes faces of children

which when the summer let them became
butterflies dallying in and out of the loft.

Morning Work

I'm up in time to see the sun strike
girders of the rail-bridge, each strut
blazing like a letter on the cover
of an illuminated manuscript
where the name of God means light.

For a second, I'm struck blind,
a man for whom the world
is a ricochet of tiny lightning bolts
that pierce to the center of the brain,
amazed how long it takes
ordinary sky to blink back.

But just now nothing is ordinary.
Six gulls pass through the shadow
of a piling, vanish, then reappear—
their wings the wake
of a luminous silken flame.

Northern Lights

They fished all day, and the boy is glad
his father knows the way through the dark.
Sprawled in the backseat, he nods
to the eerie thrum of the driveshaft,
a whir in the fingers of his limp hand
dangling to the humped floorboard.
When he sits up the night sky flickers
through the window rinsing his hands,
his skin a spackle of silver scales.
In the cooler the dead lie like shiny knives
and when he presses his face to the glass
the sky glimmers into waves
of bluegreen fire. *Look!* his father says,
It's the northern lights
and as he speaks the boy sees the future.
He's alone on the street of a distant city,
staring at the dim glitter of the stars
but thinking back to this very night,
how for a time there is no dark
his father couldn't lead him through
or call by its lovely name, if he were here.

Out of the Ruins

Fort Wright Bridge

Late in the afternoon, I climb down,
scramble loose gravel over crushed
styrofoam cups where four letters
spraypainted on the buttress
announce the American name of God.
On the abutment algae fumes in the sun
and pigeon-droppings spatter
chunks of cracked concrete
like toothpaste curdling in a sink.
If I listen to the river for long
I can't remember how old I am
and come that much closer
to hearing the forgotten meaning of my name.
Lichens gnaw into a tarnished plaque
until time is the color *1908*
and counting. I pick up small change—
raccoon bones, or a Sterno can.
Beneath the piling, in a clear pool
a fat sucker grovels on the bottom
as it lips sweet scum from the stones.

Trout

A lunker heavy in his creel,
my father climbed the steep bluff
back to our house, a rainbow

long as his forearm weighing him down.
When I flipped up the lid
patches of corruption stained its skin

like camouflage that let through flashings
of cold fire. He wanted to show me,
he said, and when I touched it

it lay almost perfectly still, its jaw
like a bellows mimicking
a dim forgotten rhythm, what made me

fill the sink, dump the rainbow in
and rock it gently so the water sluiced
its gills. I prayed for a miracle,

cried out when it shuddered
and swam nuzzling the sink-wall
in the glare of the porcelain sun.

Later, when night gleamed dark
in the center of its moon-wide eye,
I knew how far it was to the river.

Out of the Ruins

Root Cellar

The dim beam of the Everready
streaked a catacomb of dust
on the floor's dark
underside. The air matted
and thin strings of it
stuck to your skin, webs
when you brushed them off
curdling like strands of yarn.
The shelves were makeshift,
sagged rickety applecrates
leaning like a tenement
hoarding their mummied jars,
peaches like moons in fog
or forests of misted broccoli.
On the floor a smell like
old rain dried rose up,
must of russets in burlap
sacks, thin pink tendrils
sprouting like coiled antennae.
Above you, inches and a world
away, she stood at the sink
scalding chickens or scouring plates,
humming as she shifted her
weight. The oldest child,
you waited for that blessing
of dust, and it came like
rain sifted down from gaps
in the floor turned dry,
a thin silt soft as talcum
or rot from a mine's old boards
caressing your hair and hands.

Quince

for Sharon

When I saw the bruises your father left
printed on your spine like orchids
I thought of you as suddenly impossibly old,
eighteen, going on forty.

What we were flashed over me like fate,
you desperate for any hope, trying to finish
school; I so hungry for your flesh
I'd say anything I did meant love.

One night I stood by a hedge of quince
and pressed my ear to the wall
just to hear your voice wafted by the blades
of a kitchen fan, a sweet wordless chant

as you helped your grandma with dishes.
An odor of quince hung in the chilled air,
leaves like tassels of moon-spun silk,
so pale I could never have imagined

the slit a razor's edge unfolded:
that night in emergency you sat on a gurney
holding a bandage to your throat, my hurt perfected
in the glare of your love-blazed eyes.

Out of the Ruins

My Father's Work

It's a mystery how they turn to him,
silent in the ice-anointed air, these corpses
hung on their thin black chains. It's as if
his breath is a thing they remember,
the way it coils in a plume around his head,
a nimbus of warm redeeming fog. He is so tall,
he speaks from the other world, its walls
glazed with patches of frozen snow.
My own breath floats into the air
to reach his, like a cry of blood
from the ground. He lifts me into his arms,
asking me to touch one, saying *It's OK,
the skin is cold, but it won't hurt or bite.*
I press my fingers into a stiff thick flank,
its snapped ribs jutting, sawn ends
like teeth in a bloody gum.
And just then, from out in the pens
comes the sound of cattle lowing.
In the silence afterwards, I shiver
and in a gesture of love and sorrow,
my father bends and slowly lets me down.

Northern Lights

Girl and Barn: A Photograph, 1931

Blond, head cocked in a frown, she blooms
out of the drab light of the Depression,

the cigarette on her lip like a stray letter,
I for lack of a name, or an *l* for her losses

whatever they might have been.
Behind her a door opens the ripe

wound of summer, what worn slats
ask us to imagine—tang of alfalfa,

dung and old straw, that make us feel
what we want is to lie down

and be taken. A lump in the pocket of her coverhauls
may indicate the curve

of a breast, but just as easily a pipe,
snoose, gum or a pack of smokes.

The bucket at her feet carries hogslops
or a scoopful of oats for the mare, the one

she'll whisper to when the mystery
finally surrounds us, gaps in the boards

like the light between steel bars
we almost float through, dustmotes

in the chaff of a long pent sun
where the heart hangs free in its cage.

Out of the Ruins

Terminal Ice

Leaning against the door of a boxcar
Lucio lights a cigarette,
takes a slow drag and puckering
lets go a ring of blue smoke trying
to lasso the moon. Twice a minute
a search-light catches our silhouettes
on the grimy floor of the loading-dock,
two men who rhythmically lean or bend,
lumbering among forklifts and pallets.
We're too tired to know where it ends,
our work the yardman's manifest
for freight shipped to Portland, Denver.
Inside the boxcar it's dark as sin
and we feel our way by touching,
crate after crate we heave up the wall
while a hack compressor drips,
clunking an all night heart-attack.
A sickly yellow light glows
in the high window of the ice-plant
and wisps of Lucio's blue smoke
drift out over the tracks, steel rails
washed by the moon's pale light
that run through prairies of sagebrush
where snakes imitate a late night wind
and jackrabbits stitch invisible paths in the dark.

Northern Lights

Letter from Arlington
    for R.B. 1945-65

Dear Rusty,

Yesterday I searched for your name
etched in the black-lit glass
while the dim reflected overcast
made a face the shape of a soul
just losing its way. I saw it in the eyes

of a black man on the bus
coming home
from work, a look far away,
beyond resignation, beyond fear,
a blankness, drab as stone.

You knew your M-16 like a map
of the back of your hand
and may have hoped it would help you
keep the space I'm in away.
Now, we meet there anyway.

You move in a dreamy jungle rain
and the neoprene mummies appear
in a frame of the evening news,
black bags, the cold identical rows.
I stare through the letters of your name

at a ghost-face trying to find its way.
For a second the sky is burnt jungle,
then it's where I am, chilly, a trickle
I swipe from the smoky glass,
the black trees of America.

Out of the Ruins

Snapbeans

There was a green mound
heaped beyond the washtub.

When she straddled the old bench
folds of muslin spilled from under

her apron where the boy
knelt, the dark around him

like a cloak smelling of talcum
and sweat. Veins in her ankles

rose like beanvines clutching for light
and above him, muffled and intimate,

came a sound like the snap of a
slingshot, each pod delivering its sweet

split second of song. All night
the kitchen was a steaming cannery.

She'd pour the paraffin warm
to the lip of each jar, tamp the lid

and cinch it with a thin bronze ring. Deep
into morning sugar-bloom and pectin

pressed out oxygen, that *plink* when the tin
cooled, sealing her love in the dark.

II. Painting the Trim

New Year's Eve

I was driving, the kids in back asleep
as you nodded beside me.
Fat flakes of snow floated down
out of the night and were swished away
by the wipers. I couldn't see the river,
only feel it out there, urgent and black
beyond the road, its near edge
sealed by a lid of ice. Something
bolted through our lights and was gone,
the figment of a living
thing, felt, yet barely visible, that lingered
in the back of my mind and
lunged on fierce through the drifts,
beast or its ghost receding, circling.
There is no end to our separateness—
what makes us love one another
is knowing how frail and lost we are.
At the cabin, each with a child bundled
in our arms, we climbed to the loft
and those rickety web-strewn cots.
Far in the night I woke to the sound
of snow falling, a soft tampering,
lovely, indescribable. Above each cot
a dim halo of breath rose in the cold
and, lingering for a moment, was woven
with the others, then nothing if not gone.

Out of the Ruins

Floating the Salmon River

Cracked gewgaws of granite make us dawdle
as we share the oars, a diced sun

blinding us in the river's gold reflection
while a tired lock creaks for a drop of oil.

Giddy on beer, we bask in the high repose
of blue, platinum glasses shielding us

from the fiery glare. As we drift, a hawk
hangs like a floater in the lens of the sun

and we hear the slow eloquence of the current,
each inflection a glimmering silver strand. Here

is Blue Canyon, the mid-point, acme
or the door to an abyss, our sloping

middle-aged bones held up by the raft
that moves over the snowmelt summer

sluiced through deep stone dungeons carved
by a primeval flood. Call it the brooding

unpent waters of Chaos, for all we care.
When I rub you gleaming with sunblock

your skin shines like the rocks high up,
old ironwork polished by rags of sage.

Bear in Fog

A mile out on the ridgeline fog
smothers the trail, cracked talus

that clatters under our boots
and is gone. It's slow-going now

and when the fog breaks
we stare down into a meadow

where a dark shape lumbers through
patches of late melting snow,

a humped buffoon,
a sumo-wrestler in rags discovering

he's grown paws. Still more fog
and a cold endorphin-rain

say it's time to hike back—I fumble
with the camera's hopeless lens;

you smear your lips with Chapstick,
tell me *Hurry*. At twilight we grind

down the log-road in low gear.
Through the window a breeze lifts

the odor of musk and sour breath,
that greasy, bur-flecked hair.

When fog lifts, gaps in the trees
let sky back in, stars like clawtips.

Out of the Ruins

My Daughter's Song

When soft fingers of heat come twitching up
through the vents in the kitchen floor,
she begins her cooing, the click and tickle of her

consonants spliced into the purl of a vowel
as she kicks at the slats of her crib,
her bottle in a saucepan bubbling on a burner

of the stove. It's morning again—a quiet music
moves through the house and is lifted on the warming
air, and her song floats down through the bars

of the banister to the landing, dim and intimate,
like the shy duet of owl and pussycat
adrift in their moon-beamed boat,

or a leaf that fell with barely a whisper
to the river whose murmur carries it
to the stones of a distant shore.

At Dworshak Dam

My son has just left the Visitor Center,
its bright glass panels and the photographs

of men with blasting-rods and jackhammers,
dozers and high-backed trucks

hauling car-sized chunks of granite
from the banks of the mud-roiled river.

He'd been pondering a picture of the channel
jammed with slackwater, a scaffold

of girders and concrete like a hasp rising
to clamp the river's mouth shut.

And suddenly he's on the walkway running
and I hurry through the doors to catch up

but can't help imagine he's falling,
a stick-figure who kneels by the railing

then topples down the rain-streaked face
three football fields into a cauldron

of boulders and foam. But no—
he's only counting the seconds it takes

for his quarter to drop, a dot, a speck—
grit in the whipping-cream fluffed

up the side of a bowl. As we head back
the walkway beneath us trembles,

Out of the Ruins

        current slammed against the forebay
        throttled down the penstock roaring

        as turbines fire the lights downstream.
        Later, as I drive, he nods by the window,

        his face pale in the wash of moonlight
        scattered over the black water.

Fireweed

I could say his eyes as he looked
darkened like fall-ripe berries
or that pods of a tall dried weed
were bursting, the slopes flocked
with torches, each stem spurting
its fluff like smoke. But what
would it mean—that desire splits
from its parched husk, or a wind
scissors the hems of a cloud
and scatters the scraps all morning,
fall a gospel of ecological proverbs
spouting versions of the same theme,
to wit—we die in order to be reborn?
It doesn't mean a thing, but I know
my seven year old son is hurt
and amazed at the same time,
the way his eyes start swimming
as a seed-tuft drifts beyond his fingers,
when he slips off his pack
and like one relieved of body-weight
stretches onto his toes and groping
catches it, pinches the wisp
and crushes tiny nuggets of seed
he blows from his hands like ashes.

Out of the Ruins

Burning the Raspberry Canes

I've worked all afternoon
in a cool October sun
pruning dead canes and
raking them into a mound
I slosh with kerosene,
light, and after a *whump*
hear the simper and crack
as bones let go of
their ghosts. Earlier,
kneeling in thatch
I found my son's old camp
or what was left—the snapped
half of a pencil,
three rusted popbottle caps,
and in clumps of bleached
grass choking the roots of
canes, a scrap of badly
faded paper pencilled in
a child's hand, DOOR
in a dull thin scrawl and
on another up the row
sealed in a fold of earwig
husks, dim, receding, HOME.
He's ten now. I shove
the scraps in my pocket.
Fire licks the canes to
a crumble of ashen dust.
In the smoke I tear up.
For a moment I nestle in
limb-filtered light lulled
sleepy by the moan of bees.

Bouquet

for my daughter, Suzanne

Greasy and battered, the stove didn't fail us,
its jets the color of the sky
that hung like a blue tent over cedars
old as the family name.
The week was bone-dry,
rain a patter of needles
and we let the day be sufficient of its troubles
and found none. I could say
you played Old Maid or watched the ants
hauling crumbs from the table
carved with initials of lovers;
that late in the day you adopted a suicidal moth
that got ecstatic over the lantern.
Remember? I never told you
the flowers you picked were weeds—
that fistful of chicory, a stinking tiara
of cow-parsley—though indeed I wonder now.
While the Perseids hurled down fiery arrows
I managed to burn the marshmallows.
With sticks whose tips still glowed
we carved our initials out of darkness
and tricked out stars over Big Fog,
your twelfth summer, smoke on the ridge
and the road up Indian Hill, the way
your blossoms drifted Meadow Creek,
hurt in your eyes, the wilderness all ears.

Out of the Ruins

At Sheep Lake During the Gulf War

My son is happy with the trout he caught.
From the foil cocoon it baked in
he lifts a sliver of pink flesh steaming,
tastes it, and grins.
Antares scrapes the peak
and when neither of us is looking

plummets into the lake still burning.
In the coals troutbones hiss,
a whiff of rank smoke rising.
Later, in the tent my son cries out
then sinks still deeper into his dream,
like a fish near shore I startled

that lurched and swam toward the dropoff.
I conjure a prayer for my son
knowing flames roar at the wellcaps
and corpses in the sand fester
like effigies of bony tar.
There is a world I can never save him from.

But tonight what we are is here. Star-gleam
lights the beargrass to a milky bloom
and clubmoss gnaws at the shins of cedar.
The sky is a slow cortege of torches
for lives burnt out long ago,
each sparkle the name of a lovely death.

Painting the Trim

The shingles are almost Egyptian, split shakes
withering, the color of a mummy's rags.
The scaffold wobbles like an old man
whose hips are about to shatter from inside
and cotterpins squelch little shrieks of rust
like hinges in the bones of my hand.
With my brush and can, riding a plank
over twenty-five feet above the lawn,
I slap on latex black as the ace of spades
until twilight scrolls the grass, a gaggle
of paintsticks and rags, litter of Gatorade jars.
I reach for a disappearing eave, sky
dark as the long-lost bottom of my can
and down in the carport a light comes on
where my son and daughter unfold
a rickety table, string up a flimsy net
and with paddles whack at a plastic ball
kapic kapoc kapic until I rinse my hands
with thinner, the world spins to darkness
under the vast unrecoverable heavens
and love is the work
that will never in our lives be finished.

Out of the Ruins

On Finding a Snapshot of My Children

As I clean out a nook of the rolltop, it slips
from a yellowed envelope
and I find them again,
three children at the tag-end of autumn
who kneel in leafscraps after playing.

The girl in her navy sweatshirt
is just now learning to smile,
her little brother beside her
shy in his blue-plaid flannel.
Tousel-headed, short-sleeved,

the older boy
who wanted the day to be warm
leans in and touches the two
younger. The leaves lie in tatters,
old bandages suddenly set fire

that bury their denims and sneakers.
A shadow that's crawled to their laps
exaggerates the brightness behind them,
leaves glowing like cinders.
On each right cheek a crescent of light

marks its child with a tender scar,
a promise of what's too delicate to last
that holds them as the radiance waits
to fade, until I tremble
seeing how beautiful they are.

III. Obsequy for the End of the Century

Obsequy for the End of the Century

Coyoteskin

Keck says you can hear them yipping
back of his place. Says walk
until the moan of a generator
turns to a hum on the wind
and you catch it, a figment at first,
then a cacaphony of barks and
whines like the reincarnating
cries of the damned blown down
on a gust from Electric City. I make it
as far as the tackshed, but hear nothing.
Through a window on a table
splayed in moonlight, the hide
of a coyote rinsed in a tawny glow—
I enter, and slits where the eyes were
make me wonder. What are the dead
that we can touch them, that shiver
as I run my fingers over the satin
fur and looking out the window
see old Keck dumping trash
to burn in a barrel, his figure aureoled
against the snow, his hands
making a slow rhythmical motion
as he tosses something into the flames,
the sparks rising from his fingers
seen by wild eyes far away,
coyotes who just now lift their song.

Out of the Ruins

On the Palouse

The moon is down. The young lesbian
who's rented an abandoned farmhouse
sits buck naked in her rocker. She remembers
moonlight that spilled through the window,
her skin caressed by its silver fingers.

On the crest of a far hill combines
stagger over a wheatfield
like grasshoppers gorging on shoots of new corn.
She recalls a face she saw in the moon's shadow,
a stranger, her new lover.

Outside, on the clothesline, underthings
glow in moonlight and a haze of dust.
Across the gully headlights of a combine
glare like the eyes of Pharoah
searching out the last of his enemies.

Obsequy for the End of the Century

A Japanese Fisherman on the Henry's Fork

Like the emperor's robe
the river nearly blinds him.

A bright June sky no argument
against the dead, just a way

of bringing them back. Nearby
a cottonwood smokes, lint

like a light falling snow
and he remembers the black rain,

that day the horse stood melting
to its bones in the field.

When he glances at the bottom
coppering beneath his line

he tries but can't look away.
Even in a doubletake

the boulders glare
like skulls.

Out of the Ruins

Chinese Ruins on the Salmon
for Cort Conley

Spoofs of moonlight ladle the rapid as it breaks
below the bar. A latch clicks

in a hackberry bough, and I think of swallows
skittering the bluff near dark, their cries

echoing lines from *The Book of Songs*,
"I have come this far to meet you—this stream

is half-way." Pit-house walls have toppled,
basalt pried up by tourists

and dulled by a century of snow, cracks
the wind caulks, a horde of thirsty weeds.

I lie down under cold constellations, stars
marking the sign of the dragon or monkey.

Coolies staked no claim, were killed outright
or hounded out of camps named after

whores or rich ore, Florence, Stibnite.
Now the wind is a memory of opium

only the greasewood dreams, the moon a
silk-screened lantern. Rising out of clouds

it paints slow shadows on the flatirons,
brushstrokes of sage like ideograms.

Obsequy for the End of the Century

Icefishing on Lost Valley Reservoir

The lantern's so bright
they're attracted like
flies are to rot
though it's only baconfat
jammed on steel hooks
like tufts of gin-soaked
cotton a drunk smells
even in sleep. Me,
I've come for the moon
spilling its change in snow,
that high lightshow
the aurora puts on
at no charge, plush tourmaline
rainbows that mimic the
one I've laid out quivering
in a pantomime of breath.
In the bucket charcoal
simpers like bonedust.
Even in downlined gloves
my hands grasp the emptiness,
no tingle answering
the Morse of stars.
Adrift in slush the bobber
throbs its commandment—
stand, jerk hand, if there's
a tug, twist line on the
spool, if not, squat, breathe
deeply, wait. How the sky
deepens toward hinterspace,
like lights of the city
lovers glimpse from Highdrive
above instead of below.

Out of the Ruins

All those lives up there
pretending that nothing has
ended, and the dreamer absently
watching them, half in,
half out of the body,
hooked and soon to be landed.

Obsequy for the End of the Century

Steelhead

Tired of casting, hip-deep in the big river,
  on a whim I bend and scoop up
a handful of gravel, lift it in a trickle
  purling sun-stones out of my hand.
One of the pebbles shines wrong—

  a filmy, too-pink gleam, two black
dots peering from the center
  like probes. Damned if it isn't
an eggsac some female buried in gravel
  after the male milted it with seed.

I stand there, my shadow interrupted light,
  and think of fingerling and smolt,
sea-run rainbows battered by turbines,
  snagged by nets or the treacherous gaudy
hook. Bending, I try to rebury the egg,

  futile as the current slams my knees
and sprinkles a cold dash in my face.
  Bone-weary, I wade ashore, set my pole
on a rock and gaze at the failing sun.
  From here it's five-hundred miles to the sea.

Out of the Ruins

Moose

You—
plunging through the carpets of duckweed
and bluegreen algae drifting
on this quiet lake, are you so blind
you can't see me lurking with my camera
stalking your gnomelike face?
You—
so huge, so loveably ugly,
smooching your watery moss,
your snout a pendulous lobe of pry
weighted with great bone flagons,
your eyes surprisingly tiny, near-sighted,
seeing a hazy distance, the light
just dusk, your snout
a taproot sucking it back.
Now you catch my drift and lumber into
thick brush never far from water,
the hinges of your shoulders
banked on a delicate heart.

Obsequy for the End of the Century

I see us there, huddled with friends and family
near midnight in the winter yard,

bundled up for our few minutes together
in the cold. As stars spill their glitter

each of us holds a candle
and when we reach toward the center

of the glaring circle, our flames
become a single blaze that brightens.

Someone blows on a paper-whistle.
In the distance a fusillade of firecrackers.

We pass a bottle to good health and long life.
To the wheel of winter constellations

we lean close against some old despair
or take small hope

as a meteor tears a seam in the sky
then disappears in a shower of dust,

like the tail of an exclamation point
that fades under cold indifferent stars.

Out of the Ruins

The Salmon

As he grips the wire fence and gazes
into the holding-tank's long shadow
late sun fleeces his hair
and out on the river light breaks
into a billion pieces the meaning
of the word *scintillant*.
Somewhere in my son's wild heart
quicksilver is learning rose, in flashes.
"Fish," he asks it, "where are you hiding?"
and we think we glimpse it, the head
like scrapiron, fungus on its spine
like fog off the outer banks.
But it sinks back, a piece of the shadow
sucked into the bigger one below.
And speaking of below, the turbines
are thrumming the soles of our shoes,
our bodies nearly numb with vibration.
He's still looking for the salmon
when mist from the dam lights rainbows
and the spray stings our cheeks.
It is dark and I think
our journey is only beginning
and the salmon we came to see
is the life we won't get back, that sleek
silver knowing of rose and ocean
going, going, and gone.

Obsequy for the End of the Century

A Pulling
for the Katiches

Under a brittle ice-ringed moon
he clutches the jeep through snow,
searching for a bloated bellowing cow
who'd strayed so far the wind
mingled its moan with her cry,
whose calf if it were born
at all would freeze
the second it hit the air,
even before she could lick back
her steaming caul.

Late February, twenty below,
Sugarloaf a cracked skull
when he finds her, ropes her
to the jeep and slowly crawls
up the road to the barn.

In the stall, beneath a sputtering
low-hung bulb his wife
kneels beside him, the Holstein
like a stuffed overturned sofa moaning
as he rolls up his sleeve,
wraps a chain in his fist and plunges
arm-deep in her uterus
to grope for a tiny hoof.

He grunts, she triggers the ratchet,
the chain jumps taut
as it hums and the calf comes
motionless, still and blue,
eyes like bootpocks in snow.

And we leave them there, the man
trudging a snow-skiffed pen
through the herd to search for a calf

Out of the Ruins

        who can suck so her hemorrhaging
        stops, the woman straddling
        her flank, whispering
        as she strains to stand.

        And the moon above them haloed
        by the link of a chain
        that tugs toward daylight
        and one more search in the snow
        for the dead or the living,
        those still waiting to be born.

Black Lead Mountain

Where the trail climbs free of brush
and bony trunks of whitebarks,
we watch it rise, a blunt thumb
brooding over the valley,
a place last summer scarred by fire
where a boy was never found. Today
white rags skim the nape of its peak
and my son is amazed how far
he can squint through haze
toward the Bitterroots, jagged,
worn teeth clamped in a jaw. For days
Black Lead Mountain surrounds us.
We camp and fish in its shadow,
wake to a shroud of mist
where the moon has fallen.
The trunk where my son props his pack
leans like a twisted crone,
its roots acknowledging ice
and a slow indigenous burning
in the mountain's shadow,
always, only the earth.

Suicide Race
for Alex Dick

Rodeo-dust and the fluff of cotton candy.
Fried onions and the blistering noon sun.
The Okanagan winds in its bend
under willowscrub and far up the flat
the grandstand sits, a tiny doughnut

frosted with windy pennants.
In cordoned off yards of the rich,
tourists in straw hats and dark glasses
fumble Minoltas or sip mint juleps
as crowds surge toward the bluff.

Closer, in a vacant lot,
twelve riders wait on their horses,
some already drunk, one lifting a flask
to his lips, another bending
to whisper in his pony's ear ...

The modern west is a guncrack,
thunder and a miasma of dust
as they plunge the cutbank steep as fright,
one pony drowned, one rider thrown,
a bone sprouting crimson from his arm.

The winner is an Indian barely twenty
who gallops toward the grandstand
like an outlaw chased by a posse. Dust
plumes over the fairground's trampled grass,
the carnival bumped, tipis packed and gone.

Obsequy for the End of the Century

In Mountain Lightning

Huge cauliflower clouds billow and get grayer,
our skin bristling to the charge of ions

as the air starts holding its breath.
When a bolt strikes Lundy Peak

the boom three seconds later says
the storm moves faster than we can run,

our packs like deadweight, my son frightened.
A hundred yards up the trail

a bolt splits the trunk of a whitebark
and the rocks beneath us sing: *Jesus!*

I mutter, unaware of the irony,
wondering if this was the face St. Paul saw

the moment he was struck down blind.
We crawl beneath a sheltering ledge

and I hold my son close. Above us
wind roars and streaks of white light

leap over rocks like Pentecostal fire.
It doesn't matter whether we survive,

only that we're here, witness to the power
of a kingdom no less strange than this

need that makes us shiver, our backs to the wall
as we hold each other, afraid even to pray.

IV. Out of the Ruins

Passage

In memoriam Daniel Parker

That night you showed me your haybarn,
the moon swathed fields of timothy
then snagged in the limbs of a ponderosa

and hung there like a bright new dime.
Neither of us knew the cancer
had grown years, that one more spring

would turn you back into fields.
You were proud of what you'd done,
that heap of boards you salvaged

from a fire, tinscrap in a junkyard free
for the taking. It rose into the shape
that old Saxon word gave to 'barley-house,'

now home for horses, saddles and tack,
oat-bins and a corner for high-baled hay.
Your flashlight danced over rafters

like the ghost of a swallow
searching for its nest in the straw.
Happy in our new-found friendship

we stood in the doorway, sweet smolder
of dung rotting, tang of dry alfalfa.
You rolled up your sleeve and reached out

into the glare of the moon your arm,
the skin eerily pale, your face breaking
into a shy and silver-tainted smile.

Out of the Ruins

Late Autumn Run

Frazzled after work,
my nerves a bundle
of worn out shorted
wire, I change into
sweats, lace up
my Converse shoes.
West over the levee
the sun drops,
a blistering gold disc,
and shadows lean
as I run, trees
or a sloped roof
groping like claws
toward dawn. Slowly,
my body warms—
knees old doorknobs,
lungs like fists,
an old twinge nagging
my shoulder. In a yard
a boy throws a ball
an old man staggers
after. Leafscraps,
glass deckled in spangles.
From sheetmetal propped
on a garage wall
faces flash, my wife,
the children young.
Botched and in bandages
this life still shines.
A sky like cellophane,
combine glints on the bluff.
I swerve for chuckholes,
cringe at gruffs of a dog.

Out of the Ruins

Thought fragments, self
a figment—shinglescrap,
rag of tarpaper,
fust on a blackened can.
Sun is a rusted scythe.
When the pain bolts
lift-off blazes blue.
For seconds, count them,
everywhere I turn is home.

Out of the Ruins

The Elm

Armature of leaves and light, it loomed above the yard
the summer my fear set in
when to save us from a low-hung limb
that might crash through the roof in storm
I paid a man who bent with a gargling saw.
Together my son and I
heard the first great splinter and groan,
saw leaves in their windless quaking.
When it fell the earth shook hard, our breaths
stopped and we stood trembling.
On that very limb I feared, my son found the frayed noose
of a rope I'd tied on years before,
that held an old bald tire he'd swing from.
And nearby, notched in crabgrass
in a patch of trampled ground, lay the scar
his sneakers cut as he skidded braking,
dust golden, sun in his bewildered hair.

Out of the Ruins

Once each year I come back to the origins,
moss-warped slats of the porch
where a bent nail groans its elegy
and vines of a leggy rosebush bolt
through cracks in the tongue-and-groove.
Rust-gleams deify a sagging gutter
and the hallway is a grotto of charred boards
furbished by soot and morning-glory.
An appletree leans through the back door
like an ambush, the last words
of a century my breath can't escape,
deciduous, say, or *winter*. In the cracked sink
moss has wised up years after the dripping
stopped. I squint down into the cellar
through a tangle of bent pipes
to concrete bulging through spindly weeds,
the trickle where a seep runs
slick with algae, a stain
like gangrene claiming a wound.

Out of the Ruins

Hawks

Steam wisps the asphalt like lace
  from the frayed bodices of ghosts.
I brake and peel the window,

squint for a hawk on a powerpole
  beyond the old red barn, but find
only a lonely transformer hunkered

by a crosstie under a sky so dim
  it looks like another name for rain.
The engine mutters it's time to go on

but just now the face of someone I loved
  floats down out of the grayness.
This time it's nothing personal,

just the anonymous ache of regret,
  the chastening of one more failure.
We love as a way of clutching first,

and afterwards learn to let go.
  Far over the stubble a hawk is circling.
When no mice skitter out of their burrows

I pretend there is nothing to die for.
  Now the hawk dives, blood remembers:
absence gnaws this rag of a heart.

At Fishtrap

for Rich Wandschneider

A lint-flecked window, a candle in a bowl,
scrawled pages of a poem left on the table.
It's twilight. I know because the rat

who lives in the cracked stone fireplace
has stopped scratching, and the clang
of the dinnerbell that calls the others

sends me walking in gravelly dust
to the scoutcamp's old chained gate
wondering what life I can save

in words. Heartleaf shrivels on its stalk;
thistles are the spines of dead stars.
On the least wind seeds of coneflowers

scatter like eyelashes. And here come the gnats
droning hymns to the god who descends
on the last hallucogenic light, what the trees

will want to remember, gold ponderosas
whose pitch sticks to my fingers
and bristles my tongue with song.

Out of the Ruins

Workboots

I've tossed them into a closet next to
the decoys and a box of old socks,
remnants of the not-yet-thrown-away.
Funny, how when we stop using things
it's then they begin to speak, as if

what we thought was their real life
was actually a way of waiting.
They're the sad cliches of my sleep
smelling of must and linseed oil,
the smut of my corny toes. They say

we're coming apart at the seams.
We cope with resistance by carrying
our weight, and endlessly break down.
When love is finished, our tongues shrivel.
We're fed by shadows, echoes of dust, of bone.

Dragging Bottom

Near dark I stand in the river casting.
All day and not a single strike.
I've grown restless and weary
and now late shadows fall
from far trees onto the water
and I notice my line is sinking.
It's time to cash in, I think, and begin
reeling it back. But just now
there's a tug. I jerk back the rod
but it's nothing, yet for a second
a nothing that was something,
some invisible snag or rock
too far down ever to touch, or see.
And I stand there as the river laps my ankles
and wonder what black mouth waits
as the sky fades into gray,
lights of a car flicker through trees
on a road I didn't know was there
and nothing in the world has happened.

Out of the Ruins

Cedar

    In the cellar, in a far corner, there's a door
to a dying forest, its shadows etched
by the bulb of a sputtering sun.
Odor of heartwood and rain, a tang giddy
with age and distance, like cheesecloth

curing on the sill of a forgotten summer
afternoon. Garments of half-a-century
hang like festoons of moss,
her fox stole bristling to the least touch,
his topcoat, their gabardines and sweaters.

On a shelf, in an envelope marked *Mother*,
lies a shock of perfected hair,
and here is the little boat
all of you still sail in, a shoebox
whose rubberband snaps to a gritty dust,

old letters and the photographs
of small gray faces that believe
things will happen this way again,
a smile or guffaw, wave of the hand,
the hat you could almost be wearing.

Paring My Mother's Nails

When I switch off the light that hurts her eyes
the lamp on her nightstand begins
to metastasize the shadows,
the blunt shape of a Kleenex box
or the pitcher whose ice cubes I pressed
to her pus-pocked tongue.
In the hall the chatter of nurses
rings in a methodical echo,
like voices of the estranged world.
She wakes, and the light in her eyes
holds a far soft blue, like alpine forget-me-nots
I found once on a mountain trail,
orphans of cold and stone.
With a file I smooth the crown of each nail
and her dust hangs like an emulsion
I floated in once, no shadows, only the pulse
of that warm ocean. And still the lamp
casts its halo, the light grainy and dim,
like a net sifting what falls between us.

Out of the Ruins

Wildrose Cemetery

I can't fathom what calls me
in this winter twilight, a stranger
passing on the snow-skiffed road.
There isn't a soul in sight, and when
I switch the engine off wind clangs
a loose wire of the flagpole

with a din that bears no mercy,
only a ragged, intermittent pinging
that resounds somewhere beyond
what I take for loneliness or sorrow.
On the warped door of the chapel
I bang my knee, stumble over

smashed glass and find the piano
has a single working key, middle-C,
albeit a little flat, its ding
like the octave of icicles.
In *The Sunday School World*, June, 1934,
girls in virginal white gowns dance

around a maypole, flowers in their hair
the sepia of surrounding fields.
Outside, I brush the snow from a marker
and find *Eli Smith* chiselled into granite,
each letter notched with a tuft of green
where the Lord says lichens inherit the earth.

About The Author

William Johnson was born in Portland, Oregon, grew up in Washington and Idaho, taught in New York and Florida, and returned with his family in 1981 to make a permanent home in Idaho. A Thoreau scholar and poet, he is the author of *What Thoreau Said*, a critical study of *Walden*, and a chapbook of poems, *At the Wilderness Boundary*. He has won fellowships from Fishtrap, The Idaho Commission on the Arts, and the University of Montana's Environmental Institute. Johnson is married, has three children, and enjoys fly-fishing, folk-music and hiking Idaho's back country. He was appointed Idaho Writer-in-Residence for the term 1998-2001.